TEN THINGS I LEARNED SINCE BECOMING A WIDOWER

My Journey Through Grief

Gary R. Clark

Gulf Coast Press

Dedicated to all widows and widowers, and their families and friends. Those who survive, those who carry the memory...

Grief never ends…

But it changes.

It's a passage,

not a place to stay.

Grief is not a sign

of weakness,

Nor a lack of faith.

It is the price of

Love -

Author Unknown

PART I - THE LIST

GARY R. CLARK

Ten Things I Learned Since Becoming a Widower

1. There is nothing better than the love of a good woman.
2. Tattoos are permanent. Choose wisely.
3. Grief is a bitch. Make it your bitch.
4. Some of the best intended sentiments can sound so stupid.
5. It does not matter who you are, someone may be out to take advantage of you when you are most vulnerable.
6. You Learn who your friends are.
7. The grief timeline is different for everyone.
8. If there are others relying on you, you need to care for yourself first before you can care for others.
9. Loneliness sucks.
10. It's okay to cry.

GARY R. CLARK

There is nothing better than the love of a good woman

Who can find a virtuous woman? For her price is
far above rubies. – (Proverbs 31:10 KJV)

February 1981. I was living in Iowa. Two years prior, I had received my Associates Degree as well as purchased my first home, a duplex, becoming a landlord. I was four years into an insurance claims career that would span through six decades. I was twenty-six years old, and single. My older brothers had gotten married at twenty-three and twenty-one, and by my twenty-first birthday most of my high school graduating class had married. Although I had dated, there was no one seriously in my life. My family was afraid that I would remain a bachelor. I recall while getting ready for work one morning the month before, I told myself that I needed to find someone and settle down.

How did I meet Mary Lou? It began with borrowing a ladder from my next-door neighbor, Rick. He, and his wife Beth were newlyweds, and owned the duplex next door. I repaid that kindness with a cold beer, or two. Rick and I had become friends. One afternoon while I was having a beer next door with Rick, Beth had come home a little late, reporting she had been with Mary Lou. Being curious I asked who Mary Lou was. Beth worked for the juvenile probation office and knew Mary Lou from the Clerk of District Court office where she worked as a clerk in the traffic and criminal division. Beth and Mary Lou had been friends for several years, and Mary Lou was a bridesmaid in their wedding last year. Beth grabbed a photo and showed me. Now that I saw her picture, I was interested. I asked if she was seeing anyone, and it turned out to be she had dated one of Rick's friends but there was nothing serious.

I met Mary Lou in a few days when she stopped by Rick and Beth's home. I later called her, and we went to the movies on February 28,1981 to see *Stir Crazy,* starring Gene Wilder and Richard Prior. Years later we watched that movie on VHS and later DVD after a special dinner to celebrate our first date. After dating through the summer, we became engaged in September and were married on April 3, 1982. It was my grandmother's birthday, my older brother's birthday, and the birthday of my future mother-in-law.

We were happy together, although we had our struggles during the early years as newlyweds often do. We were older than the average newlywed couple of that era and we depended on our older wisdom to carry us through. We were serious about our vows to be there in sickness and in health, for richer or poorer, and in good times and in bad.

I have no way of predicting how my life would have turned out if we had not met. Some of the positives in life may not have happened had Mary Lou not been there to see us through as a couple. With her encouragement I finished my college degree, and later my professional designation for insurance claims. After first laying the foundation with a good education, we were able to move on to a newer home in our town. There's an example I use as an old Iowa farm boy when describing a successful marriage and partnership.

When you take two horses and hitch them to a wagon, and one pulls to the left and one pulls to the right that wagon does not go too far or too fast. But if they work together and pull in the same direction, that wagon begins to move along more smoothly as they work as a team. Our working together as a team helped us achieve those goals.

The 90's were a time of many ups and down for us. 1990 began with the passing of one of my best friends, my father-in-law. He died at peace after a terminal illness knowing I would be there to watch after his wife and his daughter. In 1992 we lost my mother, and my mother-in law the following year, with my dad passing in January 1999.

Mary Lou has also experienced some seizures and blackouts in early 1990, requiring her hospitalization and test. She made a recovery, although years later we wondered if those episodes were a harbinger of things to come. Mary Lou had retired from her job at the District Court office in order to be a stay-at-home mom when our adopted daughter, Jennifer was placed with us in 1993.

In 1995 I accepted a job with a major insurance company based in the western Chicago suburbs, meaning we had to move from where we spent our entire lives. That move though resulted in better medical insurance as well as better medical care, something we had no idea that we would need sooner than we thought. We found ourselves in the home where Jennifer would grow up, and it would be the last home Mary Lou ever knew.

If I could place a date on the beginning of the end that would be March 1,2001. The prior Fall, Mary Lou and Jennifer flew with me to a business meeting in Phoenix. She did not feel well on our return flight, and she had felt tired since then. Mary Lou had gone to our family doctor and received a referral to a neurologist. After he looked at her tests Mary Lou was diagnosed with Myasthenia Gravis, an auto immune disease. She had the general type, meaning that close to 75 percent of her nerve receptors were not making her muscles move. Those fewer muscles were made to work harder, and she became tired sooner.

Myasthenia was classified as part of the family of diseases under the aegis of the Muscular Dystrophy Association, and included Multiple Sclerosis, ALS (Lou Gehrig's Disease), and Parkinson's. A number of these diseases had run with more frequency in Mary Lou's family. Years later a cousin had been communicating with the National Institute of Health and that organization was interested in making a group study of her family. Sadly, that cousin had passed as well as Mary Lou.

The next fourteen years were challenging although we did what we could to give Jennifer a normal childhood and to make vacations and holidays enjoyable between the hospital and rehabilitation center stays. Although this was a rare disease affecting roughly one in 10,000, we became more knowledgeable with living with Myasthenia. Through communications online we became friends with others who had this disease across the United States, Canada, Europe, and Australia. We were resigned to the fact that Mary Lou's health would deteriorate with time. We could only hope and pray that medication and moderation could provide some stability. Remission was not possible.

We had two major setbacks. In 2003 my company has announced that it was exiting the United States, leaving me without a permanent job for over a year. In 2010 Mary Lou was also diagnosed with Parkinson's by the same neurologist who had diagnosed her Myasthenia. Mary Lou was no longer able to drive as her condition weakened and was now taxed by two diseases.

It was hard for me to be the sole wage earner as well as the housekeeper for our family. Also, raising Jennifer through the completion of her education left me with those tasks a single parent may experience. With what little help Mary Lou could provide, but with endless encouragement, we saw Jennifer graduate from high school and to receive her technical certificate from a broadcasting school in Chicago.

Mary Lou was losing mobility, now unable to climb the stairs of our home, and lived in our first floor TV room. Hospital stays became for frequent as well as rehabilitation center stays. Although my company provided excellent health insurance there were still costs that were not covered relating to her comfort and ability to survive in her environment. Mary Lou did what she could to keep our spirits up through these times. She wanted to make herself useful and continued her one activity she could still do in the mother's group at our church, knitting afghans for the newborn babies in our congregation. We had a large church; she must have knitted over 200.

Mary Lou was no longer able to stand and take any steps, even with a walker, soon after her birthday in August 2015. We had no idea this would be her last 100 days. Mary Lou would experience severe pain as her body deteriorated, needing fentanyl and morphine to such precarious levels that her breathing could cease. Our time together ended in hospice on November 25, on the evening before Thanksgiving. Mary Lou was now at peace without pain. Although Mary Lou was gone, the pain of losing her remained, as well as the void of her no longer being there.

Mary Lou was a giving person. That giving continued through memorials to our church, and the donation of her knitting supplies and yarn to keep the baby afghan project going. From time-to-time food and snacks were taken to the hospice center for the staff, and for the patients and their families.

Tattoos are permanent. Choose wisely

Early in my journey as a widower, I could not help but notice the tattoos worn by widows and widowers as a memorial to their loved ones. The wearers included children, grandchildren, and friends. There were a diverse number of styles and designs, as diverse as the wearers.

Lately, a popular type is not so much of a design, but what becomes incorporated into the tattoo. Part of the loved one's ashes following cremation are blended with the tattoo ink and applied. If the ashes are of a fine consistency and applied by a reputable licensed tattoo artist, there are no complications. You may then apply the ashes/ink combination as a portrait, name, dates, designs, or a quotation. One caveat from people who have had both this type as well as traditional ink tattoos applied, is there may be a slight itching of the newer type during healing.

Tattoos can be as diverse as the grave markers you see at the cemetery. Here are some I have seen:

- The loved one's signature.

- A portrait of the loved one

- A quote by the loved one.

- A traditional heart with the name or initials, and dates of birth or marriage or death. There may also be a ribbon underneath with some quote or sentiment.

- A logo of a branch of the armed forces, fire or police service, or a fraternal organization incorporated into the memorial design.

- Tools of the trade such as mechanic's wrenches.

- The loved one's hot rod or motorcycle, or its logo or a take on the logo. Harley Davidson is popular.

- A flower, with the name appearing in the petals, or in cursive as part of the stem, or on a ribbon tied to the stem.

- A feather that morphs into birds taking flight with a quote like, "Your Wings Were Ready But My Heart Was Not."

- Angel wings surrounding a name, Dates, or quotes.

- A favorite Bible verse.

- A butterfly or butterflies in flight.
- Songbirds, hummingbirds, cardinals, swallows, eagles, hawks, falcons, or some other type of birds.

- Firearms or fishing equipment if the loved one was a hunter or fisherman.

- A hobby, or a favorite sport such as baseball, basketball, or football.

- Musical notes and other musical symbols with a line from their favorite song.

- A Cancer ribbon or ribbon representing the disease or affliction the loved one passed from. Sometimes their name and dates are on the ribbon.

- A cross, Star of David, or some other religious symbol.

- A compass or some other type of navigational symbol.

- A hot air balloon, airplane, or another type of aircraft lifting toward the heavens.

The size may be large or small and the location may vary. The tattoo may appear on a leg, inside or outside of an arm or wrist, on or near a bosom or elsewhere on the chest, small of the back, or on the shoulder. There may also be more than one, in numerous locations.

What prompted me to include this item on the list? When I wrote the list in February 2016, I had received my first tattoo. It had nothing to do with Mary Lou as she hated tattoos. What did I get? It was a simple cursive script in black ink and reads:

"It takes a licking and keeps on ticking..."

The tattoo was placed on my upper right arm, in order it could still be covered by a short sleeve shirt. Those of you who are old enough to remember may say, "That's the old Timex® watch slogan." It reminded me of the adversity I had faced and survived during Mary Lou's illness and death, and during my own hospitalization and rehabilitation that followed. I will say that the tattoo has produced a snicker or two or a smile from a nurse while I received a vaccination or had a blood draw.

To the best of my knowledge and an extensive online search, I am certain that I am the only one with this type of tattoo. I've been asked if I had written to Timex to tell them about it. I replied, "Not yet. They'll likely write back and ask me why I didn't get a Harley Davidson tattoo like everyone else."

The following month, I received a second tattoo. It was a semicolon (;) placed on the inside of my right wrist, that could be covered by a watchband; I am left handed. What is the meaning behind a simple punctuation symbol? For me, it means survival. Traditionally, it has been a symbol for those who struggle with depression, suicidal thoughts, self-harm, or anxiety. I have told people, "A semicolon is used after an independent clause before the completion of a sentence, connecting two independent clauses. For me the sentence is my life, and I am the author. It's not over yet!"

Grief is a bitch. Make it your bitch

This may be the shortest chapter of this book, as well as the most polarizing of the Ten Things list. This one got me tossed from one widow and widower group I belonged to, although it has been endearing to the first group where I posted this list. There, it earned me the nickname as the "Grief is my bitch guy."

The point is about regaining ownership of your life. Grief will also be with you. It is about having control. It makes you think of one of those prison movies, the ones where the weakest inmate is bullied and bluntly told, "You're my bitch now!" That grieving person becomes a slave to grief, bullied and humiliated. The feeling is one of you being less than you were.

A widow friend once described the feeling to me as being off-balance. Remember those teeter totters you played on as a child? When your playmate hopped off, you were left there on your backside on the ground, feeling a sudden jolt, as well as a sense of betrayal. The only way you could find balance again to find someone for the other side, someone you can trust.

Grief is always going to be with you. The key to living with grief is to acknowledge it will always be there, while taking back ownership of your life. Make it a point to live your best life possible. You may not bully grief, but you will not let it bully you. You may peacefully co-exist with grief, but don't let it get the upper hand.

Some of the best intended sentiments can sound so stupid

Everyone says dumb things. They may not be said as intended, or they may be conveyed with their ulterior motive revealed. I am not immune from saying dumb things, occasionally afflicted with foot in mouth disease. I have said things that have been difficult and sometimes impossible to retract. Being on the receiving end is something that many of us in the widowed community have experienced.

Of all the things I and many others have heard that appears at the top of the list is "He/She is in a better place." (Like where is that place? The best place should be with me.)

There have been many more I have heard, or have been shared with me, in no order of dumbness:

- At least he/she is no longer suffering.

- Be grateful for the time you had together.

- I know how you feel. My dog (or another pet) died.

- Well, she was old. (This was remarked to me by a deacon at my church when a lady of our grief support group passed away.)

- To get over things sooner, give away or donate all his/her property. You don't need any reminders.

- Don't have so many pictures of him/her sitting out.

- Stop wearing your wedding ring. You'll scare away potential dates.

- What are you going to do?

- Will you be selling the house?

- Where will you live?

- Was there insurance?

- How much does the funeral cost?

- You're young and can remarry.

- You're getting older and should not be so fussy about your next partner.

- You're not getting any younger. You better get out and meet someone.

- Everything happens for a reason.

- You need to stay strong.

- How are you able to stay so strong? (Like, do you have a choice?)

- You can lose yourself in your work.

- You were his/her caregiver for so long. Now you can rest.

- Were you left financially secure?

- It could be worse.

- Do you ever wish you could trade places?

- You'll feel better in time.

- You'll find someone else.

- Pull yourself together.

- Put on your big girl pants.

- You are not alone.

- Call if you need anything.

- You need to find someone to be a mother/father to your kids.

- At least all your kids are now grown.

- Your children are so young that they won't remember.

- You should be doing better with no more medical bills.

- I don't think I could survive my husband/wife passing. I'm glad it happened to you, and not to me.

- How are you?

- Do you think you can get married with so many kids?

- You have a lot of kids to be there for you.

- I didn't even like my wife/husband.

- You were expecting this, weren't you?

- How long are you planning to be grieving? Get over it.

- God doesn't give us more than we can handle.

- There are people who have it worse off than you.

- It's time to move on.

- It's a long hard road.

- It was his/her time to go.

- I admire your strength.

- Give it a year.

- Why have you started dating already?

- Why haven't started dating yet?

- You really shouldn't consider dating anymore?

- So, you're single now, huh?

- His/her spirit will always be with you?

- What do you think he/she looking down from heaven is thinking about you, the way you are now?

- God did you a favor taking him/her away.

- If you get married again, you'll no longer be a widow/widower.

- Your dead wife/husband would be disappointed by the way you're acting.

- You've been making some dumb decisions.

- You're grieving wrong.

- What's wrong?

- You'll see him/her again someday.

- Don't you think it's time to move on.

- Stop dwelling on things.

- You should do okay with that negligent death lawsuit.

- God has a plan.

- God needed him/her more.

- Are you going to keep all these pictures up?

- He/She is at peace now.

- Are you looking forward to getting back on the market?

- What were his/her last words?

- Suicide doesn't have the stigma it once had.

- You don't look old enough to be a widow/widower.

- Aren't you a little young for this?

- Aren't you glad this happened closer to the end of your lif

- You must have had things rough. You look older than you are.

- You sure have let yourself go.

- If you're getting lonely, you know where to find me.

- Some people never get married. At least you did.

- It's easier to love a widow/widower than a divorced person.

- You're lucky. My ex-husband/ex-wife is still around.

- It will pass.

- I remember how hard it was when I was going through my divorce.

- Stop posting about your grief. You're embarrassing the family.

- You act like you're the only one who lost someone.

- The Lord works in mysterious ways.

- I bet you feel dumb for being religious as you are after this happened to you.

- At least it was him/her and not you.

- He's not really gone. He's watching over you.

- I wish my husband/wife was dead so I could get the Social Security survivors benefits.

- Things will get better with time.

- I feel sorry for you. Things can only get worse.

- Time heals all wounds.

- At least you weren't married yet.

- That saved you the hassle of a divorce.

- One good thing about him/her dying, look at all the weight you lost.

- Are you relieved?

- Heaven needed another angel.

- It's the circle of life.

- Sorry we can't make it to the funeral. We're going on vacation. We'll call you when we get back.

- Now that you're alone, can you house sit, and pet sit for us while we're on the cruise?

- I'll make you an offer on that lake house you won't be needing any more.

- It is what it is.

- Life goes on.

- You should see a counselor.

- When are you going to feel better?

- We can't make the funeral. We have tickets to one of those Irish dancing shows.

- How long are you going to talk about this widow thing? It's been six months and I'd like to talk about me now.

- Sorry to hear about Jimmy, but you'll meet someone and next time make sure he has money.

- At least for the next time you learned from your mistakes.

- Why are you wearing your wedding ring? You'll scare away the prospects.

- Get over it. He/She is never coming back.

- You must have said or done something to bring this on.

- You were too good for him/her.

- I feel your pain.

- Your husband/wife would have been married by now if you had died.

- God took your husband because he was a smoker and was going to get lung cancer, so it was better for him to die of a brain aneurysm.

- You're better off; he/she was so sick.

- You remain here for a purpose.

GARY R. CLARK

After you've seen all these things that are so wrong, what can you say that will be the right thing? That list is short. Short is easy to remember. You could say:

- I don't know what to say.

- I am sorry for your loss.

- I can't imagine what you're going through.

- Take time for yourself.

It does not matter who you are, someone may be out to take advantage of you when you are most vulnerable

With changing times and technology, let's change that "may" to a "will." I have sadly learned about too many occasions where this has happened. One time is one too many. Taking advantage of those in a weakened or vulnerable condition has been ongoing since Biblical times.

> *They take advantage of widows and rob them of their homes, and make a showing of saying long prayers – (Mark 12:40 KJV)*

This has happened to many; it has happened to me. It can even happen before or soon after the funeral when the widow or widower is at their lowest, in a fog and most vulnerable. Suddenly cash, jewelry, or other property is found missing from the home. Money is requested for certain expenses for the funeral or estate business only to be found to have been diverted elsewhere. In the meantime, "friends" and neighbors may even come to raid the garage or shed "reclaiming" loaned tools and equipment.

There may be life insurance payments, litigation awards, cash settlements, or other windfall monies that suddenly find adult children, even those estranged, siblings, and others close to you, want a piece of the pie. This may be in the form of loans which are never paid, or outright gifts of money or property.

Stepchildren may surface and there may be animosity as the late spouse is no longer there to act as a buffer. There may be intimidation or the threat of suits. The presence of a large sum of money and a sizable estate can bring out the worst in some people. Sadly, surviving spouses have been evicted by the deceased spouse's children who were left the family home in the will. A stepmother may suddenly find herself homeless with nowhere to go. She may have contributed to the furnishing of that home. There are often comingled assets including cars, bank accounts, and other real estate that may only appear in the decedent's name. A widowed spouse may experience a change from a comfortable life to becoming impoverished in as little as 30 days. Often the domestic help and service providers are treated with more courtesy.

It does not stop with family, friends, and neighbors. There may be credit card companies, medical collections services, bill collectors, and insurance companies to deal with.

Remember the scene from the Ryan O'Neal movie, *Paper Moon*? O'Neal played a Depression era traveling Bible salesman and conman who would search local obituaries, then show up at a widow's doorstep to deliver a Bible with her name engraved in gold, stamped with equipment he carried in his car. He would provide a high-priced C.O.D. invoice in her late husband's name, explaining that her husband had ordered it as a gift for her. In almost all cases the widow would pay without question.

That con still exists in modern times in different forms. In one city a furniture store, upon waiting for a week or so after the funeral would have a driver arrive in front of the widow's home with a recliner and a C.O.D. invoice in the late husband's name. The driver would explain that her husband had special ordered a recliner for her before he passed. Because it was a special order, the store cannot send it back to the factory. The good news is the store attempted to practice this chicanery too many times, and the owner has been prosecuted for fraud.

If you are a widow or a friend or family member of one, you or someone you know may fall victim to a scammer on social media, providing attention that that the receiving party has been missing. Some of these people are very shoddy in their presentations, while some are very detailed in setting up their profiles. Several years ago a widow who lost her husband in a boating accident less than two years prior, asked me to check into a man who claimed to be a petroleum engineer for a major oil company on assignment in Poland. I reviewed his Facebook page and profile. He reported to be based in Houston. Through an additional search I discovered a petroleum engineer for the same major oil company, several years younger and based in Dallas. Now, what would be the odds that a major oil company would have two petroleum engineers with the same exact name, and both were based in Texas? The younger engineer's profile was more detailed because it was the legitimate one. The widow was able to report the scammer to Facebook and block him. That doesn't do much to alleviate the dashed hopes or the embarrassment or humiliation.

How did I get into the avocation of helping widows ferret out scammers and hustlers? It may have started with my background in fraud and arson investigation for the insurance companies I worked for during my career. Our special investigation unit occasionally ran seminars on mining data on social media. Everyone has the potential to be a victim, including me. Especially me.

It can happen early when we're in a fog, commonly called widowed fog, though also known as griever's fog. We may still be processing the loss and attempting to comprehend the present. My early experience was not with a scammer, but with a real person, a friend of a friend who reached out to me, knowing I was lonely and in a vulnerable state. It was discovered that her motive was to seek a job recommendation as she was currently unemployed. Desperate times call for desperate measures by desperate people. I have also seen members of the widowed community solicit for funds and help from fellow widows and widowers.

How can you protect yourself? Several reputable authors and counselors suggest placing yourself on a restricted budget. You can spend your money how you wish but at least for a while, have a trusted friend as a sounding board for any expenditure, for example over $100. You can still handle routine expenses on your own such as the mortgage or utilities. You may feel defensive at first because you are not a child. You are in a fog, though. As time passes you can always raise the limit and later remove the restriction altogether. You will not regret parting with that money.

You learn who your friends are - Or, Everyone needs a Larry

I have seen it happen. I have experienced it. A loved one passes. Neighbors bring food over. A family member or friend goes with you to the funeral home to make the arrangements. The bereavement committee from church arrives with a hot meal and to finalize the details of the funeral Mass. You go over the details of the service including the music, the readers, and even the funeral luncheon. There is a lot of food on an occasion like this. And you can't remember most of it.

The day of the visitation at the funeral home arrives. You greet friends, family, and co-workers as they stream through to pay their respects. The following day is the funeral at church. At the conclusion, the funeral director took the casket containing Mary Lou to Iowa for the memorial service to be held in three days. Those remaining walk down the hallway to the parish hall for lunch. I visit with family and friends and give Jennifer a goodbye hug as she heads for the train back to Chicago. Afterwards a friend and I stop at the local Chili's to have a margarita. We talk about when he used to come to our house down the block in Iowa and have one at the bar in our basement, calling it "scurvy medication."

I am dropped off at the house, I enter the front door, and then it hits me. I look at the plants sent home with me earlier, and realize for the first time since Mary Lou passed, I am alone. That's it. No one else will be there. I walk back to the TV room where Mary Lou spent the last two years of her life. It is more like a hospital room with its bed, oxygen equipment, and the supplies and medications. It was a stark contrast to the room where we watched TV, sat by the fire, and celebrated birthdays and holidays.

I climb the stairs to our bedroom. Mary Lou had not slept in our bed for over two years, no longer able to navigate the stairs. Mobility was limited to only where a wheelchair or walker could go. I rarely slept here as well, keeping a single bed in the TV room so I could be close to her to tend to her needs.

I don't recall everything that happened in the next two days. The fog was settling in. I can't remember how I slept that first night. Saturday had me packing clothing for the Monday service in Iowa and calling my fried Larry to discuss the itinerary. He and his wife Gail were going to pick me up at the house and stay Sunday evening at the casino hotel near the funeral home and cemetery. I had decided that since it was early December and as Iowa winter weather was unpredictable, we would have all parts of the service including the graveside portion inside the funeral home.

I can't remember much more about Saturday, except watching the Iowa Hawkeyes in an early bowl game. Their playing was dismal, but that was the least of my worries. During the night I found myself getting up to go to the bathroom with increasing frequency. This continued all night as I continued to feel weaker and feverish. Fearing dehydration among other things, I threw a few things in a bag and called 911 at 6:00 a.m. Sunday morning. Remembering the difficulty that the EMT's had with running a stretcher up and down the stairs on a prior call for Mary Lou, I went downstairs to wait for them. I'm not accustomed to riding in an ambulance, the last time was about 25 years before after an auto accident.

While in the emergency room, I informed the staff I had to be in Iowa the next day to complete Mary Lou's burial. They told me that I was not going anywhere soon. That admonition was supported by all the tubes and wires connected to me. I was diagnosed with a bladder infection, blood infection, kidney stones, and a temperature of 102. An IV kept me hydrated and it was not until the next day I could hold food down. Later in the day I called Larry to tell him where I was. He and Gail went on to Iowa and together, with our friend Brian, and with one of Mary Lou's cousins took care of the service at the funeral home. One of Mary Lou's cousins, also with Parkinson's had made the trip from San Francisco. I did not want to delay things for her or others. Larry settled the bill with the funeral home on my behalf as it was unknown when I could be back there to handle business.

I was feeling beaten down at the lowest point in my life. Mary Lou had just died, I was in the hospital for the first time in my life, and for the kicker it was likely someone close to a family member had wanted me dead. As bad as I was feeling, I gathered enough resolve to disappoint that person.

After spending several days in the hospital, now able to walk with a walker, and eat on my own, I was transferred to the same nursing and rehabilitation center where Mary Lou had stayed several times, including three weeks before she passed away. The staff was surprised to see me as a patient, especially the administrator who I met with during Mary Lou's last stay. The rehab stay really gave me a boost. I was in better health, but mentally still in a fog.

It was going to be at least a year before my health returned to precrisis level. Part of the journey included what became four kidney stone procedures, known as a lithotripsy. I was to be placed under general anesthesia and needed to have a driver. That is where my friend Paul stepped in. He was a retired engineer from a telecommunications company who with his wife Cynthia had attended our church. They had six adult children, sadly one of them passed. Paul and I were first acquainted when he assisted Mary Lou and I as a substitute driver when we ran the church owned bus to transport children to a local parochial school.

Paul was also my sponsor for RCIA (Rite of Christian Initiation of

Adults) when I decided to join the Catholic church. In 2013 Paul had been my driver after I had a skin cancer procedure that had required a general anesthetic. Paul liked barbeque, and I did too, and I had to fast before each procedure. On the way home we would stop and enjoy some barbeque.

Let's go back to my friend and former neighbor, Brian. He was our neighbor up the street when Mary Lou and I lived in Iowa. He was on the police department as well as an EMT for a private ambulance service. His medical prowess came in handy as Mary Lou had some health episodes in the early 1990's before she exited the workplace and became a stay-at-home mom to care for adopted daughter, Jennifer. We had remained friends over the years. In late October 2015 Brian had come to spend a couple days keeping an eye on Mary Lou in order for me to have a respite break. When he arrived, he saw Mary Lou in her hospital bed, and went to his car to retrieve his kit and checked her vitals. Noting her weak state further declining, he called 911 and the ambulance took her to the hospital. Brian drove me there, stopping on the way at a local burger place to grab a bite to eat, as the paramedics told us that it would be nearly an hour before we could see Mary Lou in the Emergency Department. It was going to be a long night ahead. When we entered, I recall seeing the menu board, and it was like seeing something for the first time. For the first time in months, we were going to sit down and eat. I had felt so disconnected the past several years, limiting my trips to work, church, and the grocery store, I had the feeling that I was just released from captivity and was returning to society.

We arrived at the hospital as Mary Lou was being processed in the ER. The ambulance was later than expected as the paramedics needed to stop on the way to stabilize her condition. Brian and I had discussed Mary Lou's condition as very grave. I still had no idea that she would be gone within four weeks. He admonished me, and wisely advised me, that I should be taking better care of myself. Caring for Mary Lou, working a fulltime job, and running the house was taking its toll on me.

When Mary Lou passed, he played a key role with Larry, tending to Mary Lou's memorial service and her burial when I was in the hospital and could not be there. We have maintained our friendship to this day. Several years ago, when I needed to have an outpatient test that required me to be under a general anesthesia, Brian was my driver to the hospital and back home. Without having a driver as well as someone to watch my post-test condition, I would have not been allowed to have that test.

How did I first meet Larry? It was about 2009 when I was working in downtown Chicago, adjusting property and heavy equipment claims for one of the world's largest insurance companies. Larry owned an auto and heavy equipment independent claims adjusting company that serviced the Midwest and other areas. We were meeting for lunch to discuss a file about a large generator engine that was accidently dropped in the sub-basement of the Sears Tower. Larry had also previously handled claims for me before for construction equipment as well as farm equipment.

He was a couple years older than my oldest brother. His family had been in the service station business, owning a Standard Oil station at a key location in the early days of O'Hare Airport. Larry had a colorful past. He had played football for Northern Illinois University until a car accident injury sidelined him. Through an owners' group, he became friends with the son of another station owning family. As Larry had a boat, he and his friend were dating several bunnies from the Playboy Club in Chicago. He met his wife of over fifty years, Gail, who had worked for one of the airline executives at O'Hare. She was Miss DuPage County® at the time. They met when she brought her pageant automobile into the station to have a mechanical issue checked out.

Through his work and connections performing tasks for salvage sellers, Larry had occasion to acquire salvage property including high-end jeans, jackets, shirts, and accessories that had recovered in a claim for a store in Arizona. Knowing I had experience with eBay® sales, he told me that he was having trouble moving the merchandise through garage sales. I was able to list and sell Ralph Lauren, Levi's and other brands across the country and in several continents. Little did we know that load of merchandise would result in a profitable business partnership.

After Mary Lou passed, I needed to make some sizeable repairs to our home, including the replacement of the furnace and air conditioner. Our next project involved bidding on old sock merchandise shelf pull lots on auction from Amazon® and acquiring the inventory of an insurance claim for a boutique in Indiana. We hit paydirt in March 2017, acquiring an entire semi load of close to 10,000 pieces of major department store merchandise that was rejected when the transporting semi-truck tipped over. I had started selling upscale handbags and ladies clothing on eBay, barely making a dent on the load, and advised Larry that we may need to break the load into bulk lots for sale to dealers. We had some seasonal goods here and the ladieswear could fall out of fashion.

That's where my friend Maggie came up with an idea. She asked if we would consider selling merchandise on consignment. I approached six stores in Illinois. Although those stores occasionally received new goods, they had not received larger quantities in the variety, styles, and sizes we had to offer. We were able to move the truckload, the boutique, and the Amazon merchandise within the year. More about Maggie later.

Larry and I continued to find new salvage and overstock merchandise over the next several years. In the meantime, I had sharpened my marketing and merchandising skills. When I retired in Spring 2021, Larry wanted to curtail his activity having just celebrated his 80th birthday in January. We struck a deal and I bought him out. I also assisted him with his insurance claims adjustment business, employing my marketing expertise as well as my technical insurance skills. In August Larry was hospitalized and I watched the business for him.

While attending a car show several weeks later, I received a call from Gail. Larry had passed away that morning. I had lost my best friend. Again, there was a feeling of loss. Except for his time in the hospital, we talked every day. Working with his daughter in Arizona who performed his bookkeeping and accounting tasks, I was able to assist the family with the discontinuation of operations and the closing of the business. I had remembered what Larry and Gail had done for me when I had been in the hospital and could not complete Mary Lou's burial and was honored to be of help.

I recall telling a widow friend about Larry and how he came to help without a question during the darkest time of my life. I will always remember her reply, "Everyone needs a Larry."

Now, more about Maggie. I met her when I posted on a Facebook page for widows and widowers I had recently joined in January of 2016. I had told that Mary Lou had passed on the evening before Thanksgiving. I had suffered not only the shock of losing Mary Lou, but I was also recovering from my hospital and rehab stays. I had missed Thanksgiving, Christmas, and New Year's and I was not going to let another holiday slip by. I posted that I would send a Valentine's Day card to any widow who wanted one. The offer resulted in me sending out over 20 cards, including one to Maggie. I had learned that she had lost her husband of seventeen years, John, in a daytime multiple fatality accident, the fault of one of the other drivers. Maggie was left to raise her eleven-year-old son by herself. She lived about 40 miles away and we later agreed to meet for lunch. We became immediate friends. Maggie told about her experiences following John's death. She had recently incorporated her business, with plans launch services for the widowed community. She had written material after meeting with accountants, attorneys, funeral directors, and other professionals who interacted with the widowed community as part of her business. Her goal was to offer resources and services to those businesses as well as to the widowed community.

Over the years Maggie has become a trusted friend and advisor, even assisting me with her knowledge and expertise in human resources, as I had experienced several post-loss issues at my work. She was also a sounding board for ideas Larry and I had for our side hustle. Maggie's business has now evolved to include the Widowcoach © Facebook page and website, as well as published materials to assist the widowed community and their families. As I write this, she is co-author of an anthology, The Voyage & The Return: The Path to Self Discovery. The joint effort has received excellent reviews while making several best sellers lists on Amazon in multiple countries. Without Maggie's encouragement I don't believe I could have written this book.

The grief timeline is different for everyone

How long does grief last? I don't know. I heard that grief is something that will always be with us. There are those who imply that the most severe part of grief can last from six months to four years.

It can begin before the death of a loved one; often called anticipatory grief. During the time of a long or terminal illness anticipatory grief can occur. That happening does not shorten the timeline; in fact, it may extend the overall time.

That does not mean that the loss of a loved one who passed away from a lengthy illness was more severe or painful than for the person who lost someone due to a sudden death or accident. I have been told by mental health professionals that there is no comparing of grief. Loss of life experienced by one person is often not more or less significant than the loss experienced by others. Grief may arise from other events than the loss of a loved one. There may be the loss of a marriage, a pet, health, security, a home, or a job.

Grief and loss can affect others different ways. I remember a local plant that as part of workforce reduction had offered early retirement. In the next eighteen to twenty-four months there were an increase of obituaries in the local paper of early retirees from that plant. In contrast, there were other retirees from the same company who spent many active and happy years together having parties, playing golf, and even meeting up as snowbirds in Phoenix during the Winter. Mary Lou's uncle was in that second group. Was grief experienced over the change in employment status a cause of death for that first group? I don't know, but the events could be connected.

I witnessed another example of loss in my early years of working as an insurance claims adjuster in Iowa farm country. There was a house fire for an older couple, a total loss, what we may refer to in insurance as a grounder. There was really nothing left except a pile of debris and ashes. I recall sitting with the farmer and his wife, and our inspector at the kitchen table at a son's farm. The farm wife was visibly shaken. Their home was lost. She had spent her entire married life there. It was the center of her life. She raised her children, and later her grandchildren, and celebrated every holiday and special occasion there. Any reminders of her life were gone. I explained the claims process, the coverages, and the payments. Construction began on a new home, a modern ranch style for suitable for an aging couple. The farmwife was still upset. Within months of moving into their new home, she had passed away.

I have also experienced the opposite. There was a fire at another farmhouse several years later. A younger farmer met me in the front yard and showed me inside in or for me to begin my investigation and assess the damages. In the living room I noticed and overhead light fixture, filled with water from the firefighting activity. I couldn't help but recall the Three Stooges short film where Moe, Larry, and Curly were building a house, and the light filled with water when the light switch was turned on. I discretely kept my mouth shut. The farmer happened to have looked up at the same time and remarked, "You remember that Three Stooges episode when the water filled up the light?" "Yeah, now that you mention it."

I guess it's how you look at it. One thing I learned from my career is that things are just things. It is the safety of the people and their well-being that is most important.

There has been reference in different citations what is called the five stages of grief. Although additional studies and research have proven this to not apply to all. Elisabeth Kubler-Ross had first addressed those five stages in her 1969 book, *On Death and Dying.* Those five stages were placed in order as:

1. Shock or denial
2. Anger and guilt
3. Bargaining
4. Depression and sadness
5. Acceptance

Let's refer to these five stages as parts, going forward. Often appearing with the shock of the death of a loved one is the denial that it happened. I can remember when Mary Lou passed away although I cannot remember all the details. There was a numbness. This condition commonly may be called a "widowed fog" although professionals will call it a griever's fog. It has been explained at times that this is a way the body can protect the mind and the heart.

I can confirm that this happened to me. When I was in the hospital just two days after Mary Lou's funeral, I gave no resistance to the numerous tubes or leads that were attached to me, as well as the syringes for blood draws or vaccinations. Mary Lou had always teased me about being needle shy. I didn't remember any pain. That numbness remained with me as I got a tattoo about eight weeks later. This fog has been reported to have been present for an extended length of time for one year to eighteen months. Sometimes it may never go away and will remain to some degree. Forgetfulness often comes with grief and will affect short term memory.

This fog should not be confused with PTSD (Post Traumatic Stress Disorder). This condition may occur when the grieving spouse was a fellow passenger in a transportation accident or was witness to the homicide or suicide of a loved one, as well as other circumstances of loss.

I can attest that the anger is very real. It has been pointed out to me. I was angry that Mary Lou was gone, I landed in the hospital, and for all the mess I was left behind in the form of being physically, emotionally, and financially broke. I constantly reminded myself that I was faithful to Mary Lou and had kept my promise to be there for better or worse, for richer or poorer, and in sickness and in health. I went to work to rebuild my life and my health although it took several years to work through my anger. Through the years I have observed anger in others. It is something that needs to be addressed and handled if there is any hope for a future relationship.

What is bargaining? This may be the shortest part that you may experience. It may result in a misdirected hope in the face of inevitable tragedy. Bargaining may also be the most internal stage, closely followed by depression. You may attempt to make a deal with yourself or with God to be a better person, or to behave better. You may also think about the "what if's" and wish to go back in time in hopes to at least improve the situation.

Depression may often be the most confusing part of grief or grieving. Within four months of Mary Lou's passing, I was having problems staying focused and I was struggling at work. I contacted my company's Employee Assistance Program after discussing my situation with Maggie, my widowed friend who had an extensive HR background. I went to see my doctor first before applying to EAP, aware that others with my problem had been prescribed medications to help, as well as to receive a referral. Upon taking a battery of tests, I was told that I was still grieving the loss of my wife. Although I was truly sad, I did not suffer from depression. With my referral, I received eight one on one counseling sessions per year over the next several years.

Some of these four parts may not appear at all, or in any order, or all at once. They may even disappear and then may resurface again. There may be triggers, either conscious or subconscious. A visible trigger may be visiting the gravesite or going through old clothing or possessions. You may find yourself avoiding a certain restaurant, activity, or vacation destination that you most enjoy. I have found myself avoiding a certain drugstore because that was where most Mary Lou's prescriptions and medical supplies came from. There are even several brands of foods preferred by her that I avoid. A subconscious trigger may be a date on the calendar, or a certain song coming to mind. I have compared notes with others in the widowed community, and we discovered sometimes having a down day and later noting it was for example a Wednesday, or the 25th of the month. It is like there was an internal clock to remind us.

Acceptance is considered as the final part of grief, although it does not mean the end of grief. It means that you are facing without denial the reality of your loss. It does not mean that you condone what happened; you are accepting that the event happened. To arrive at this point, you will need to take as long as you need to take. I have been told that you cannot go around grief, you must go through it. Having often hearing that I was reminded of the old spiritual:

> So high you can't go over it
> So low you can't go under it
> So wide you can't go around it
> You must go in at the door.

The grief timeline "is" different for everyone. I personally believe that I have reached this stage. I cannot tell you how long it took me, but I have accepted the reality. Again, it does not mean that grief is gone from my life, it means that I am able to live with it. The moment of acceptance can be compared to when you go to sleep at night. You cannot tell the exact moment when you fell asleep last night, but when you wake up in the morning you know you did.

If there are others relying on you, you need to care for yourself before you can care for others

When I first wrote my list, the first thing that came to mind was being seated in a passenger jet, waiting for take-off. The flight attendants are at their assigned stations, pointing to the exits, instructing how to use the seatbelts, and orientating the passengers for procedures in the event of an emergency. Finally, each holding an oxygen mask, they demonstrate when one drops down from its compartment overhead. They instruct you that if you see someone nearby who needs assistance to first put on your own mask before you attempt to help others.

You need to look after yourself, even at times all you are responsible for is yourself. Good health is an investment. Good health keeps you energized. Good health keeps you working. The fruits of your labor pay the bills.

Regarding money, you need to take care to avoid becoming the ATM of Mom or Dad. Maintaining control of your finances is crucial especially in the early days of your widowed life. During that time, while you may be in a fog, it is too easy to part with assets, especially cash. I know of one widow who was financially stable following the death of her husband. She was left with the home and no mortgage, life insurance, savings, and no bills. She had two adult children, both married and with their own households and families. Although they were working, those children were aspiring to the lifestyle they experienced while growing up. They were needing money for a remodeling project, lessons or activities for the kids, or an emergency that they had not saved for. At the end of her days, that widow had sold her home, dispersed the cash, was down to her last several thousand dollars, and living in her daughter's basement. The widow had a heart condition; you would think that at the least she would be given a room on the ground floor.

At times you need to ask for help. That is nothing to be ashamed of. Are you receiving the resources that may be available to you? If you are working, does your company have an Employee Assistance Program (EAP)? If they have this program, do not hesitate to take advantage of it. There is also a level of confidentiality here; your manager will not know you participated.

If you are an AARP member, there are numerous health and financial tutoring resources available that come with your basic membership. There are numerous community outreach programs; one is located down the street where I currently live in my town of less than 5,000. Do you belong to a group of widows and widowers, single parents, or retirees with similar circumstances? Sometimes, it does take a village. Asking for help is not a sign of weakness. You do need to vet your helping resources.

Consistency, rules, and boundaries are crucial. At the very least having them in place lend to the stability and security of the home environment. Your children or others in your charge or care know what is expected. Unscheduled events or expenses that could hemorrhage cash in the family budget are less likely to occur. As you set these rules, show your love, support, and encouragement. Be receptive to talk about death and loss when questions or comments arise. Your children are close to the loss as well; this was a life-changing event for them, too.

I tend to visualize the loss event as a pond. A stone is dropped in the middle, symbolizing the death or loss. You are closest to the middle and experience the most severe wave. Your children are close as well and experience a rough wave. Other family members and friends are at different locations and experience waves of varying degree. Finally, the waves become ripples and turn into calm waters.

Loneliness sucks

This is a tough topic. It is also one that as phrased contributed to me being booted from a widow and widower group. You can still be surrounded by people, yet still feel lonely. It is not the number of people in your life, but the quality of friendships and relationships. Who is in your circle of friends? Who in that circle share a part of your life outside of work, school, church, or some other organization or activity?

Loneliness can even exist in a marriage when both partners have drifted apart. Friendships can also change, common interests change, as well as changes in family obligations, work, or when friends move away.

There can be a combination of factors contributing to loneliness from losing your spouse, and some of them are because you lost your spouse. The two of you may have socialized with other couples. After the passage of time, you attempt to rejoin the group, although things don't feel right. There is an odd number of people now and the odd one is you. You may receive a cold shoulder or the silent treatment. Invitations to dinner, shows, or other get-togethers may diminish or disappear completely.

You may have been the primary caregiver for your spouse during a chronic or terminal illness. You cannot get out and socialize, and the only people you come to know on a regular basis are medical professionals and service providers as well as hospital, care facility, and hospice staff. These are some of the nicest and kindest people you will meet, but they will disappear when your loved one dies.

You may still be working. That environment can vary. You may own a family business, or work for a small company in a small town. The work dynamics change with the size of the company. I experienced this when I worked for a small mutual insurance association in Iowa. We all knew each other and each other's families. I later worked for and retired from one of the largest insurance companies in the world. I commuted from the western Chicago suburbs to a high-rise in the Chicago loop. We had people from Wisconsin and Indiana also coming into the office daily. These were nice people but someone occupying the desk next to mine could be living over 75 miles away. We may visit over and occasional lunch, but they were not coming over to the house like my colleagues in Iowa did.

In the years before Covid our team worked remote when conditions allowed. During Mary Lou's final months, I was thankful that I could work exclusively from home as she needed more attention. When she passed and we had visitation at the funeral home near where I lived there were new team members including my first manager who I met in person for the first time, coming to pay their respects. There was also a lady from my office who sat down near me and conveyed her sympathy. I was still in a fog, trying to remember who she was. I am glad that I did not embarrass myself by asking. I later remembered that she sat less than 30 feet away from me at the office. I would like to say that after retiring and moving twice including back to Iowa, that I maintain contact with most of those people. I don't.

Loneliness can vary depending upon what stage we are in life as referenced my prior work life. There may be a greater disconnect in some organizations. Having people around us and near us can have a positive coping effect. At the end of the day, you are often alone. It's that social support during the workday that helps you get through the entire day.

While caring for Mary Lou during her long-term illness, I became almost as isolated as her. There were immediate family members who we had not seen in years. Friends and neighbors also move away. As our daughter grew there were parent groups that we were involved in that were no more. We were knowing fewer and fewer people.

We are an increasingly transient society. We hardly know our neighbors. Take this test: How many of your current neighbors can you name? How many people do you know from work? From church? From the health club? At what generation in your family do names and faces of your blood relatives begin to become unfamiliar?

I had asked myself that question after Mary Lou had passed. I discovered that I was so removed and disconnected from almost everyone I knew. How was I going to fix this? One of the first things I did was accept invitations. Even if I didn't think that I wanted to go or was afraid to, I went. At least I got out of the house, sometimes meeting people I hadn't known before. It was a bit awkward at first, and sometimes a bit uncomfortable but I went. If someone was having a grand opening for a laundromat, I was there.

I discovered that I was on to something. While reading about retirement as well as the widowed life, I noted multiple references about maintaining my social circle and becoming socially active. "Get out and get around" became my motto. The older you get one thing is certain. One other certainty is if you don't continue to grow your circle of friends as others move or pass away, the more likely you are to end up alone. Imagine this: your eighty-something self is going to the hospital or the nursing home. You are asked for an emergency contact and cannot provide one. This happens to more people than you think.

What can you do to combat loneliness? I see lists of suggestions. I don't believe that any one suggestion will be a one-size-fits-all solution. One of the most frequent suggestions is to volunteer your time and your services. I read an article on retirement today that reported that if you did not perform any volunteer work before you retire, it is less likely that you will after you retire. If you do volunteer, find a cause that you can get behind and believe in, the more transparent it is in organization the better. What part of the organization resources supports administration, and what percentage benefits the intended beneficiaries? Treat this the same way you would research a charity when making a monetary contribution.

Regarding charities and non-profit organizations, beware when you pick up the phone. That friendly sounding voice on the other end of the line is a professional fund raiser who wants your money. They are trained to ask you the right questions to get you to open up about yourself to establish a rapport and are willing to trade their time with you for your contribution to their cause or charity. Many elderly and isolated people find themselves parting with substantial amount of their money in exchange for a few moments of attention.

Being lonely and starved for attention can be how widows and widowers who are starved for attention fall victims to the scammers on social media, posing as doctors, members of the military, or engineers and contractors who are stationed overseas. They create a story of their own loneliness. It is easy to portray. How many times have you seen those ads on TV or in a magazine for the USO, supporting reaching out to servicemembers overseas? Although USO is indeed a worthy organization deserving support and contributions, there are those who use the scenario for less than honorable means.

If these people are busy where they are stationed, how do they find all the time to message you? Shouldn't they be working at what they are stationed there for? What time zone are they located? And if they have such a great job, why do they need money?

What are other things you can do to combat loneliness?

- Join a club or group of those with similar interests or hobbies or pursue a new interest.

- Join a gym, take a fitness class, join a team, or just take a walk. You may be surprised who you meet along the way while improving your health.

- Adopt a shelter animal or become a foster parent of shelter animals before they can be placed in a permanent home.

- Keep your mind sharp while attending a seminar. You can refresh, update, or learn new skills. My computer background dates to the Ford administration. Updating computer skills is on my personal list as well as taking refresher courses in history, science, and economics.

- Check the local community college for different craft and skills programs. I joined a writing and self-publishing seminar which kickstarted me to complete this book. In addition, from joining a writers' group at the local library, I had a sounding board for future projects.

Do what you like and what works for you. Finding a way to overcome loneliness may have the side benefit of restoring your physical, mental, and emotional health.

It's okay to cry

We all do it. It's part of what makes us human. Our Lord and Savior, Jesus Christ even did it. It is memorialized in the shortest verse of the Bible:

Jesus wept. - (John 11:35 KJV)

Jesus was grieving from the loss of his friend, Lazarus. He was weeping in sympathy for the loss suffered, not only his own but the loss to Lazarus' family and friends.

I am the worst when it comes to crying or not crying. Over the years I lost my parents, grandparents, other family members and friends. I hardly remember shedding a tear. Maybe it was my faith. I truly believed any suffering was over, and my loved ones were at peace in heaven. I also believed that the best way to honor those who passed was to keep it together and tend to and comfort those who appeared to be more shaken than I was. I soldiered on, tending to whatever needed to be done. Call it conditioning. I maintained a stoic appearance, even when I was alone.

This worked until August 2019. In June, I had sold the home we had together in Illinois those final twenty years that Mary Lou was alive. We bought it when we moved for my work. It was where our adopted daughter, Jennifer, grew up. Mary Lou was gone, and Jennifer moved to Oregon. I decided to downsize, selling our home in June, moving to an apartment, as well as experience a change of scenery, those last few years before I retired. In my job as an insurance claim adjuster, I was fortunate to perform most of my work at home, and I relocated to a town fifty miles to the north, and still on a trainline to downtown Chicago.

Earlier in the week I had seen my grief counselor. During our last session she had asked me to write a letter to Mary Lou, telling what I had been doing since she passed. My counselor was aware I had some anger issues over what had occurred in the final years of her illness and life, as well as my circumstances up to the time I had sold our home and moved. The uninsured costs Mary Lou's illness and other expenses left me financially taxed at her passing, and for several years following. I refused few things she wanted, even though I would be alone to experience the consequences. How do you say no to someone who was going to die?

Many things were broken and in disrepair in our home. Due to her autoimmune disease, we could not have workmen come in to make repairs. This same illness prevented many visitors from coming to see us, resulting in our lonely existence. My time in the office was decreasing, as well as the time I could socialize with people outside our home. My time as her caregiver increased. I was to the point of exhaustion and landed in the hospital within 48 hours of her funeral. The anger I harbored had been with me for over three years.

At the appointment my counselor was surprised to see me pull out a composition notebook with a 25-page letter. She remarked most of her clients usually wrote only a page or two. I read the letter, taking over 30 minutes, and we discussed it for the remainder of the session. I had felt as if a great weight had been lifted from me. I went to sleep that Tuesday evening, experiencing one of the best nights of sleep since Mary Lou passed. I was expecting a similar experience for the next evening. Boy, was I wrong.

I woke up from a sound sleep about 4:00 a.m. Thursday morning, sobbing and crying uncontrollably. I remember thinking that the only one who loved me or would ever love me had died, and I felt so lost. This went on for over two hours. I had to begin work shortly. I cleaned up, grabbed some breakfast, and logged on to my laptop for the day's work. I kept a box of tissues close by, finding myself tearing up during and after client calls.

I called my coach, advisor, and friend, Maggie. She talked with me at length about my loss, and listened as I read the letter, and suggested that I needed time to process the anger and grief that the letter had allowed me to express for the first time. It's normal and natural for grief to encompass all the emotions, including anger. I had been under tremendous stress as a caregiver for years and I was now at a point where I could express the emotions from that time. Crying was normal and natural and a stress relief. I needed a break in order to regroup and recharge.

I had called my manager and placed *out of office* messages on my phone and email. I took some Tylenol and set my alarm. When I awoke later in the afternoon, I spent a quiet evening at home. This has not happened to me again. My experience was a lesson to me to not keep things bottled up inside. It was okay for me to let my guard down. It was okay to cry.

GARY R. CLARK

PART II - MORE THINGS

GARY R. CLARK

Grief Trilogy

Morning

Stumble down the stairs
Slipping and tripping, head throbbing
Made way to the kitchen
Stark light hurts red eyes
Fill coffee for her in her favorite cup
Trembling fingers fail
Drops to the floor and shatters into a thousand hot pieces
Ear is poised to hear
"Hey honey, what's that noise?"
But there is no voice
That voice died, and your spirit died, when she died.

Mid-day

In the office
Stark light hurts red eyes
Stack of papers growing taller
Boss wants to see you one more time
"What's going on with these open files?"
"And shouldn't you return those calls?"
Back to the desk, slump into your chair
Stark light still there
Check the calendar, oh hell
Anniversary was two days ago
Pick up the phone and drop it, remembering
The only anniversaries will be those in your mind.

Evening

Walking to the station in the rain
Forgot your umbrella

The wind and rain cuts through to your soul
If you had one
Beer girl shakes her head and almost questions as she says
"Three tall boys again today"
Home, to add one more pizza box to the stack
Beer can pyramid crashes with a clatter
Look in the kitchen
Stark light still there
Dirty dishes too
Tired tonight will do them tomorrow.
What is tomorrow?

What I Miss

That start of the day. Everyday. The small talk, those little exchanges before we go on our way. Never parting without that hug, that kiss, and "I love you." Knowing we will be back together and looking forward to the time we are together again.

What I miss

Sitting across or beside each other in a restaurant. Holding hands, looking into each other's eyes. No need for phones. It's our time together.

What I miss

Together time in the car. Off for a day trip or a weekend adventure. Our catch-up time of the week. Every minute is our time, together.

What I miss

Our time together in the world. Family, friends, anyone, cannot say one of our names without saying the other. They know we are inseparable. They know us for the love we have for each other. There feels like there is a light that is given off from our love.

What I miss

Holidays. Christmas, Valentine's Day, even Arbor Day. Always a reason to celebrate our love for each other, and our time together.

What I miss

Building a life together. Trusting each other with our lives, our fortunes, and our hearts. I take care of her and she takes care of me. And realizing and appreciating that our lives together are so much more than life alone.

What I miss

That time at the end of the day. We talk about our day. We listen to each other, caring, really caring what has happened. Knowing that what happens in our lives affects each other. And not wanting it any other way.

What I miss

Our time together at night, whether at home or traveling, it's always the same. A sameness and a togetherness and an intimacy and a love that we cherish. And we nurture it and watch it grow. And the caring and the tenderness. And the assurance when the morning comes we are there for each other. And if either of us wake during the night, there's that little touch, that little kiss and back to sleep. For the best sleep ever.

What I miss

Stuck Here in Chicago Without You

As the cold wind burns my face,
In this Godforsaken place,
This damn weather chills my soul the whole way through.
I wander a dark street,
Feeling tired, feeling beat,
And I'm stuck here in Chicago without you.

I sense the stinging sleet,
Dirty slush is at my feet,
As the world turns a sullen jail-like hue.
There's an emptiness inside,
That appeared the day you died,
And I'm stuck here in Chicago without you.

I now arrive alone,
At a place I once called home,
My clothes are soaked,
My heart now broke in two.
Sunny days have come and went,
Replaced by Winter's discontent,
And I'm stuck here in Chicago without you.

I Saw Her Picture

I saw her as a child, a beautiful child, without a care, playing with her brothers and sisters, with hope of good things for the future.

I saw her picture.

Cap and gown, or uniform. She came from New York, West Virginia, or Texas, or Chicago, or California. Ready to face the world and the future. Confident, young, beautiful. As a nurse, a teacher, in business, or in the military. Ready to act, ready to serve, ready to love and be loved.

I saw her picture.

As a beautiful young bride on her wedding day. With a young man who without a doubt was the luckiest man in the world. With all the hope and the promises of the future ahead.

I saw her picture.

As a young mother, holding her own beautiful child. There is no mistaking the care and the loving in her eyes. And later, you would see this same care and loving, in holiday photos, family gatherings, anniversaries, and trips. You knew what her treasures were.

I saw her picture.

At the funeral, at the cemetery. The despair. The feeling of hope and the future slipping through her fingers. And all she ever did was love someone with all of her heart and all of her soul, forever.

You see the eyes, still on the verge of tears at any moment. You see that attempt at a smile. You see that love for those around her. Grief cannot take away love.

You know that you cannot know how she feels. You know only of your own pain, of your own loss, of someone who loved you more than anyone. For the rest of her life. And then her life ended. You cannot know, but you can understand.

You feel like you want to reach out and hug her, and wipe away her tears, and tell her things will be all right. But it takes more than that to make things all right.

At times all you can do is pray for her future, and for those close to her. And pray that grief does not destroy her or those near her.

You pray for a renewal, for health, and happiness, and for peace. And then you say a little prayer for yourself.

I saw her picture.

You're Not There

When we were young
We had not a care.
It is different now
You're not there.

The touch of your lips
The softness of your hair
Is just a memory,
You're not there.

The world we knew,
The love we share,
Is forever gone,
You're not there.

Life Began with You

Life began with you,

A new world, a new beginning filled with hope
and promise

With everything we do.

We would start our lives together with love,
tenderness, and care

Built upon a solid foundation of the love that we
would share.

Life would grow with you,

Every day was bright and new.

With you as my friend, my partner, my
love, my wife

We had the best in our own world, The
best in our own life.

Life ended with you

The life that we both
knew.

Death may try to separate us

Though love will not keep us apart.

As I travel alone in life's journey

Holding you forever in my heart.

I Sit by my Window

I sit by my window endless days
Just watch the world go by ever since you
went away
Don't even know if the sun is in the sky
Doesn't really matter ever since I had to say goodbye.

Days turn into months and the months turn into years
I lose track of time between the sorrow and the
tears
Every moment is a battle
Every hour is an uphill climb
Seems I have no purpose but to sit here marking time.

I lie awake alone through endless nights
I just stare through the silence since you got your wings, and you
took flight
If Hell is dark and cold, then it's surely where I must be
There I remain since the day that you left me.

I sit by my window endless days.

At the End of the Day

The morning's here, the sun comes
up
You're at the table with your coffee
cup.
That look in your eye, the smile on your face
It's a moment in time I would never replace
And I smile
And I know it's with you
I want to stay
At the end of the day.

It's a hard day at
work
I start to feel blue
I reach in my heart for a memory of
you
And I smile
Now it's time to go home
I'll be on my way
To be with you
At the end of the
day.

In the glow of the moon
I see your smiling face
I feel the warmth of your kiss and your loving
embrace,
And I smile
And I thank God for this wonderful life
I was blessed the day you became my wife

And it's here
I want to stay
At the end of the day.

The Crossroads of your Heart

Life has left you beside a long and lonely
highway,
You lost your way
You don't know where to start.
You move along with grief as your
companion
Until you find yourself at the crossroads
of your heart.

You stop to rest
And there you meet another
Someone who knows the pain of a broken
heart.
You talk awhile about life's lonely journey
At that forsaken place
The crossroads of your heart.

It is time to leave
As you must be traveling onward,
A new companion,
Together, you set out, a new start,
As you leave behind grief's heavy burden,
At a place that's called the crossroads of your heart.

I Owe a Widow

One Sunday morning as I was getting ready for church, I thought about the months and years since Mary Lou passed away. I thought about the fog I was in; my life was a mess on all counts. I did not like myself at all, and I doubt that anyone would like me the way I was behaving, or not behaving.

I think about the progress I made since then. I've seen improvement in many parts of my life, but I have a confession to make… I did not get here by myself. I had help and guidance from someone who had suffered the worst loss of her own life, a widow. Not just one, there were a number of these amazing ladies who steered me in the right direction. They all saw something in me that I was failing to see in myself.

In the early days, there was the first widow I met through a blog that she ran. She lived in the UK, six time zones away. When I would wake up in the middle of the night, she would be getting ready for work. We would message back and forth. She would head off to work, and I could get back to sleep. We still communicate on occasion. She has now been engaged to a fortunate gentleman who will have the privilege to spend the rest of his days with her.

There is also the widow who had suffered the loss of a husband as well as a son within weeks of each other and had her own missteps in her life. She knew I was very vulnerable but would keep an eye on me. She is a trusted friend today.

There is the widow who recognized my writing talent, giving me encouragement, and was that voice that is still inside my head providing me that encouragement.

There is the widow who encouraged me to think about what is possible, to not only to be able to do just one thing, but to do several things, and strive to do them well.

There is the widow who had her own Facebook page for the widowed community. She recognized that I was behaving badly, and it seemed out of character for me. She would have my back. She would be my conscience, almost like Jiminy Cricket sitting on my shoulder.

There is the widow who had suffered great loss on multiple counts, including the loss of her husband in a tragic accident. Then she met her new love, and he died of brain cancer five years later. Through it all she wanted to help others who had also suffered the loss of a spouse. She helped me and became one of my closest and most trusted friends. I am happy to report that she has launched a successful enterprise for service to the widowed community.

There is the widow who lost her husband about the same time I lost Mary Lou. She reminded me that I tended to overthink at times. To this day, when I find myself overthinking about some matter, I am reminded of her words. I am happy to report that a good gentleman who treats her with all respect due to her, is now married to her.

There is the widow who I always told that she was the girl I wished I had met in high school. She helped me find my way back to where I was, my most authentic self, living a life that is truer to who I am and who I want to be. She is still one of my best and most trusted friends.

There is the widow, who although she had suffered great loss of her own, had kept a joyous spirit, and professed great faith. She was concerned about my mortal soul and had prayed for me. I cannot explain it, but I found myself getting back to church and reading the Bible, something that I had strayed from.

There is a widow who has suffered great loss on many counts, including the loss of her husband. She was always optimistic and had taught me to appreciate what I had in my life, and to be thankful.

There is a widow who has also suffered great loss, including the loss of her husband. Although faced with great adversity, she always has a smile on her face. Even though she was faced with many tasks ahead, she has taught me to take time to enjoy life, enjoy friends and family, and to enjoy the beauty of the world, no matter where that place in the world may be. She taught me to smile.

There is one more widow I cannot forget. She had lost a husband in the war but found the strength to persevere. She married a farmer from Iowa who was back from the war. She was my mother. If she had not taken the journey she had, I would have never been born. She gave me life, and a mother's love.

I have so much to be thankful for. I owe a great debt to these kind, and generous, and beautiful ladies who have helped me find my way on my journey.

Afterward

I was reading remarks by a widow who was wanting to get away from it all, wanting to start over. To rediscover who she was and to reinvent herself.

I thought about what had happened when Mary Lou had passed in November 2015. And the changes that had come from her death and she was no longer with me, at least physically.

And I look back at what I was left with physically, mentally, and emotionally. The final years and months of her illnesses and her passing left me heartbroken and battered.

I think of the stories of others in the widowed community, and your tales telling me what you were left with. Many of us were left all alone, to deal with the loss of the ones we love, and other issues as well. It was one giant hurt with more hurt piled on.

I remember early on as issues arose, thinking, "Was this a part of the widowed life, or part of a regular life?" After some time, I thought, "What difference does it make?" I need to deal with those things no matter how they happened. It was all part of my life now going forward.

It's hard. It's hard for all of us. From that day forward when our loved ones died, we had to deal with the events of life, and often do it alone.

I am amazed of the accounts some of you tell, of what you made happen. Life is not better but improved from where you started after your loss. You were able to bring some joy back into your life, and to the lives of those close to you. It's encouraging. It gives hope for others when you tell your story.

Here's hoping that your story will include new beginnings, reinvention, new hope, new life, and if you want, new love. We all understand what you have been through. We all understand that you are deserving of all good that may come your way.

This book is for you.

Acknowledgements

Writing and publishing is a team effort. There were beta readers and several friends who provided that extra set of eyes, as well as their valued opinions about content. A special thanks goes out to Annie Bernard, Mona Guedry, Brian Guy, Allie Larson, and Joyce Roling.

Although I am not a professional in the matters of grief and loss, at times I needed to consult a credentialed professional in order to be certain that my observations still were correct. A special thanks goes out to a great friend, Maggie Moore, also known as The Widow Coach. You can find Maggie and information about her services on her Widowcoach page at https://www.facebook.com/thewidowcoach

Finally, this book could not get to press without a consultant, someone who has blazed the trail. I have known Roxanne Boersma for several years, after taking her self-publishing seminar at McHenry County College, as well as from a local writer's group at the Cary (IL) Public Library. Roxanne is an experienced tech-savvy consultant, having successfully self-published over 15 titles in several fiction genres. Her service information is available at www.SistersRomance.com/consultant.html or email at RKBoersma@SistersRomance.com

About the Author

Gary Clark grew up on a farm in Iowa, the state where he received his education and began his insurance career. After they were married, Gary and his wife Mary Lou and their adopted daughter Jennifer, made their home in the Chicago area where he worked for two global insurers. After Mary Lou's death and his retirement, he returned to Iowa. Gary enjoys music, road trips, and attending car shows.